CONTENTS

Introduction

The Foodi is pretty cumbersome and has a current and sturdy look. It additionally comes with a truthful few accessories to deal with the unique sorts of cooking, including a 2d lid for strain cooking. Don't expect this to be clean to shop, but its well worth bearing in mind that it's far designed to update some of kitchen home equipment, so it'll prevent area on this respect. The controls are very truthful and intuitive to use, even without the recipe guidance. Just choose the placing you want, and regulate the time and temperature with the arrow keys. Ninja got here out with the Foodi that is an electric powered stress cooker that is unique in that it addresses a grievance many humans have approximately pressure cooking; that it's tough to create crunchy ingredients or a crispy-on-the-out of doors-moist-on-the-internal product. In addition to strain cooking and slow cooking, the Ninja Foodi OP three hundred additionally air fries crisps, bakes, and broils, sears, and sautés meals. This approach which you have to be able to pressure prepares dinner a hen after which crisp the skin all in the identical equipment.

About Ninja Foodi Grill

Even within the most organized and spacious kitchens, it's tough to make room for unmarried-motive countertop home equipment. So frequently you'll use a product a handful of instances, most effective to relegate the cumbersome one-trick pony to the closet, the attic, or maybe the tag sale. But products which could do multiple issue, and do them nicely, perhaps worth giving a permanent domestic for your countertop.

The most modern device clamoring for space? The Ninja Foodi Grill, one of the most recent additions to a developing environment of Foodi merchandise. In addition to grilling, it is able to also air fry, bake, roast, and dehydrate. Here's the lowdown on whether it's really worth the large greenbacks it's presently selling for—or whether you'd be better off with any other one of our favorite indoor grills.

The Ninja Foodi Grill is huge and it's boxy—7 inches long with the aid of 14 inches wide with the aid of 11 inches tall. To give you an idea of just how massive that is, believe an all-in-one printer, or a completely big bread field. The grill is built of brushed stainless steel and has a black plastic domed lid.

With the grill, you get a hefty grill grate, a crisper basket, and a cooking pot which can be all lined with a ceramic nonstick end. A cleaning brush and kebab skewers also are protected.

As you may think, this Foodi can grill. Although it cooks with the lid closed, the lid doesn't press down on food, so it simplest brands grill marks on one aspect at a time in case you want a Panini, you'll have to turn it over midway thru cooking. The grate leaves curved grill marks rather than immediately lines on food.

In addition to grilling, the Ninja Food Grill can air fry, roast, bake, and dehydrate, which overlaps with a number of the functions of the Ninja Foodi Pressure Cooker and Ninja Foodi Oven.

What you will like

It's well built.

The digital controls are easy to study and intuitive to navigate.

It's first rate at grilling—and it doesn't produce smoke.

It is also used for air frying, roasting, baking, and dehydrating.

PROS

Easy to include it to your cooking ordinary

The interface is person-friendly

Air frying function

Dehydration feature

Available in sizes

Dishwasher secure add-ons

14 degrees of protection

Tender-crisp technology

Keep warm up to 12 HRS

CONS

The most important lid is not removable

It is heavy and tall

In stress cooking mode, the air frying lid stays open

Steam launch valve operates manually

The cable could be a chunk longer

Dehydrator rack is offered separately

Breakfast Recipes

Low-Carb Breakfast Casserole

prep times: 10min **cook times:** 15min **total times:** 25min **serving:** 8

Ingredients:

- 1 - LB Ground Sausage
- ¼ Cup Diced White Onion
- 1 - Diced Green Bell Pepper
- 8 - Whole Eggs, Beaten
- ½ Cup Shredded Colby Jack Cheese
- 1 - Tsp Fennel Seed
- ½ Tsp Garlic Salt

Instructions:

1. On the off threat that you are utilizing the Ninja Foodi, utilize the sauté potential to brown the frankfurter inside the pot of the foodi. In the occasion that you are utilizing a Ninja Foodi, you could make use of a skillet to do that.
2. Include the onion and pepper and prepare dinner along with the ground wiener until the vegetables are sensitive and the hotdog is cooked.
3. Utilizing the 8.75-inch container or the Air Fryer skillet, splash it with a non-stick cooking bathe.
4. Spot the floor wiener mixture on the base of the skillet.
5. Top uniformly with cheddar.
6. Pour the crushed eggs uniformly over the cheddar and frankfurter.
7. Include fennel seed and garlic salt uniformly over the eggs.
8. Spot the rack within the low state of affairs within the Ninja Foodi, and in a while region the box on the pinnacle.
9. Set to Air Crisp for 15min at 390 levels.
10. In the occasion which you are using an air fryer, place the dish legitimately into the bin of the air fryer and cook for 15min at 390 tiers.
11. Cautiously expel and serve.

Nutrition Information:

Calories: 282 **Fat:** 23g **Carbohydrates:** 3g **Sugar:** 2g **Protein:** 15g

Cast-Iron Scrambled Eggs

Prep/total times: 25 min, **serving: 6**

Ingredients:

- 12 - large eggs
- 2 - Tbsp water
- ¼ teaspoon salt
- ¼ teaspoon pepper
- 2/3 - cup finely chopped sweet onion
- 1 - jalapeno pepper, seeded and chopped
- 2 - Tbsp butter
- 1 - log (4 ounces) fresh goat cheese, crumbled
- 3 - Tbsp minced chives

Instructions:

1. In an enormous bowl, whisk the eggs, water, salt and pepper; put in a safe spot.
2. Spot a 10-in. cast-iron skillet on Ninja Foodi oven broil rack over medium-hot warmth. In the skillet, sauté onion and jalapeno in margarine until delicate. Include egg blend; cook and mix until nearly set. Mix in cheddar and chives; cook and mix until eggs are totally set.

Nutrition facts:

Calories 217, **fat** 16g, **carbohydrate** 3g, **protein** 15g.

Prosciutto Egg Panini

Prep/total times: 30 min, **serving: 8**

Ingredients :

- 3 - large eggs
- 2 - large egg whites
- 6 - Tbsp fat-free milk
- 1 - green onion, thinly sliced
- 1 - Tbsp Dijon mustard
- 1 - Tbsp maple syrup
- 8 - slices sourdough bread
- 8 - thin slices prosciutto or deli ham
- ½ cup shredded sharp cheddar cheese
- 8 - Tsp butter

Instructions:

1. In a little bowl, whisk the eggs, egg whites, milk, and onion. Coat an enormous skillet with cooking splash and spot over medium warmth. Include egg blend; cook and mix over medium warmth until totally set.
2. Join mustard and syrup; spread more than 4 bread cuts. Layer with fried eggs, prosciutto, and cheddar; top with outstanding bread. Spread exterior of sandwiches.
3. Cook on a Panini producer or indoor Ninja Foodi oven broil for 3-4min or until bread is seared and cheddar is liquefied. Cut every Panini down the middle to serve.

Nutrition facts:

Calories 228, **fat** 10g, **carbohydrate** 21g, **protein** 13g.

Ginger-Glazed Grilled Honeydew

Prep/total times: 25 min, **serving: 6**

Ingredients:

- ¼ cup peach preserves
- 1 - Tbsp lemon juice
- 1 - Tbsp finely chopped crystallized ginger
- 2 - Tsp grated lemon zest
- 1/8 - teaspoon ground cloves
- 1 - medium honeydew melon, cut into 2-inch cubes

Instructions:

1. In a little bowl, join the initial 5 fixings. String honeydew onto 6 metal or drenched wooden sticks; brush with a large portion of the coating.
2. On a gently oiled rack, barbecue honeydew, secured, over medium-high warmth or sear 4 in. from the warmth just until melon starts to mollify and brown, 4 to 6min, turning and seasoning oftentimes with residual coating.

Nutrition facts:

Calories 101, **fat** 0, **carbohydrate** 26g, **protein** 1g.

Eclairs on the Grill

Prep: 5 min. **grill: 5** min. **/batch, serving: 6**

Ingredients:

- Wooden dowel (5/8-inch diameter and 24 inches long)
- 1 - tube (8 ounces) refrigerated seamless crescent dough sheet
- 3 - snack-size cups (3- ¼ ounces each) vanilla or chocolate pudding
- ½ cup chocolate frosting
- Whipped cream in a can

Instructions:

1. Set up an open-air fire or Ninja Foodi oven broil for high warmth. Wrap one finish of a stick or wooden dowel with foil. Unroll sickle mixture and cut into six 4-in. squares. Fold one bit of mixture over the readied stick; squeeze end and crease to seal.
2. Cook over open-air fire or Ninja Foodi oven broil 5-7min or until brilliant earthy colored, turning at times. At the point when the mixture is sufficiently cool to deal with, expel from the stick. Get done with cooling. Rehash with residual batter.
3. Spot pudding in a resealable plastic pack; cut a little opening in one corner. Crush pack to squeeze blend into each shell. Spread with icing; top with whipped cream.

Nutrition facts:

Calories 293, **fat** 12g, **carbohydrate** 43g, **protein** 4g.

Snacks and Appetizers

Crockpot Chicken Taco Dip

prep times: 5min **cook times: 5 HRS total times: 5 HRS, 5**min, **serving: 9-10 cups**

Ingredients:
- 1 - pound chicken breast
- 1 x 16 ounce can refried beans
- 3 - cups salsa
- 8 - ounces reduced-fat cream cheese, softened and cut into 1" cubes
- 2-3 Tbsp McCormick Gluten-Free Taco Seasoning
- ½ - cup nonfat plain Greek yogurt
- 1 - cup shredded pepper jack cheese
- 1 - jalapeno, sliced
- corn tortilla chips for serving

Instructions:
1. Spot chicken bosoms at the base of your moderate cooker. Spread with beans, salsa, cream cheddar, and taco flavoring. Cook on low for 4-5 HRS, blending once in the middle of if conceivable.
2. Evacuate chicken and shred. Take about a Tbsp of warm dunk and blend into Greek yogurt to temper, at that point add Greek yogurt and mix to consolidate. Mix in destroyed chicken. Move to a stove safe serving dish and top with destroyed cheddar. Cook on sear until cheddar begins to brown and air pocket, around 3-4min. Watch cautiously to abstain from consuming.
3. Top with cut jalapeno and serve quickly with chips. Extras might be refrigerated in an impermeable compartment for 5-7 days.

Nutrition facts:
Calories 249, **fat** 5g, **carbohydrate** 29g, **Protein** 23g.

Crock Pot Margarita Chicken Dip

Prep Time/Total Time 1 hr 10 min, **serving: 12**

Ingredients:

- 12 - oz cream cheese, softened
- 1½ cups chicken, cooked and shredded
- 2½ cups Monterrey Jack cheese, shredded
- ¼ cup tequila
- ¼ cup lime juice
- 1 - tbsp lime zest
- 2 - tbsp fresh orange juice
- 1 - tsp kosher salt
- 1 - tsp cu min
- 2 - cloves garlic, minced
- A small container of Pico de Gallo

Instructions:

1. Cut the cream cheddar into little shapes and layer over the bottom of a medium-sized stewing pot.
2. Spread the destroyed chook over top of the cream cheddar and unfold with destroyed cheddar. Add the relaxation of the fixings to the sluggish cooker.
3. Turn the simmering pot on high, unfold, and heat for approximately an hour or till the plunge is warmed via. Mix the plunge some instances as its miles warfare ming up to mix the fixings and protect the base from cooking.
4. Serve heat with tortilla chips and pinnacle with Pico de Gallo.

Nutrition facts:
Calories 186, **fat** 3g, **carbohydrate** 17g, **Protein** 24g.

Hot Caramelized Onion Dip

Prep time 10min **cook time 2 HRS 30**min **total time 2 HRS 40**min, **serving: 6**

Ingredients :

- 2 - large onions, halved and thinly sliced
- 2 - Tbsp butter
- 1 - Tbsp canola oil
- ½ teaspoon fresh thyme
- 1 - Tbsp granulated sugar
- ½ Tbsp balsamic vinegar
- 4 - ounces cream cheese
- ½ cup sour cream
- ½ cup full-fat mayonnaise
- 1 - cup milk
- 1 - Tbsp minced garlic
- ½ teaspoon red pepper flake
- ¼ teaspoon black pepper
- ¼ cup parmesan cheese
- ½ cup brie, diced
- 1 - cup shredded gruyere

Instructions :

1. Warmth the oil and spread in an enormous cast-iron skillet over medium warmth. Include the onions and let sauté for 5min, mixing as required. Include the thyme and sugar and keep on cooking for 20-25min on medium-low warmth. Make certain to mix the onions each 5min so they caramelize equally. In the event that anytime the onions are caramelizing excessively quickly, turn down the warmth to the low setting. Add the balsamic vinegar to deglaze the dish, permit the onions to absorb everything. Expel from heat.
2. Shower within your moderate cooker with cooking splash so the plunge doesn't adhere to the sides. Include the caramelized onions, cream cheddar, sharp cream, mayonnaise, milk, garlic, red pepper pieces, dark pepper, and parmesan. Permit the plunge to cook, secured for 2 - 2 ½ HRS on the high warmth setting. Check and mix as required.
3. At the point when 40min stays in the cooking time, include the diced brie cheddar and mix to consolidate.
4. At the point when 20-25min residual, include the destroyed gruyere top. Remember the gruyere won't earthy colored and air pocket in the moderate cooker. It will anyway dissolve and become tacky. For a bubbly top, move the plunge to a buttered heating dish, at that point top with gruyere, and permit the cheddar to dissolve under the oven for a couple of min.
5. Serve warm with toasted loaf cuts or wafers.

Nutrition facts: Calories 106, **fat** 6g, **carbohydrate** 3g, **Protein** 1g.

Ninja Foodi REUBEN DIP

prep times: 10min **cook times: 2 HRS 30**min **total times: 4 HRS 40**min, **serving: 10**

Ingredients :

- 1 - (8-ounce) package cream cheese, softened
- 1/3 - cup mayonnaise
- 1/3 - cup Thousand Island Dressing
- 1 - Tbsp milk
- ½ - pound thinly sliced deli corned beef, cut into thin strips and then chopped
- 1 - (14.5-ounce) can sauerkraut, squeezed dry in paper towels
- ½ - teaspoon Worcestershire sauce
- 1½ cups shredded Swiss cheese

Instructions :

1. In a medium bowl, combine cream cheddar, mayonnaise, Thousand Island dressing, and milk. You needn't bother with it totally blended or smooth; however, get the cream cheddar separated a few.
2. Mix in outstanding fixings.
3. Move to a delicately lubed stewing pot or a simmering pot fixed with a slow cooker liner.
4. Spread stewing pot and cook on LOW for 2½ HRS, mixing part of the way through.

Nutrition facts:

Calories 298, **fat** 23g, **carbohydrate** 6g, **Protein** 18g.

Slow Cooker Bacon Cheesy BBQ Chicken

PREP TIME 15 min **COOK TIME 2 hrs TOTAL TIME 2 hrs 15** min, **serving: 12**

Ingredients:

- 12 - Schwan's Fully Cooked Bacon Slices chopped, divided
- 1 c. - Schwan's Diced Chicken Breast Meat
- 1 c. - milk
- 1/3 c. - shredded Mozzarella cheese
- 2 8 - oz packages cream cheese, room temperature
- 2 c. - shredded cheddar cheese
- 1 - Oz pig Ranch Dip Mix
- 1/3 c. - BBQ Sauce
- 2 - Tbsp chopped green onion

Instructions:

1. Combine all ingredients besides 2 slices of bacon and green onions in Slow Cooker.
2. Cook on low for two-3 HRS; stirring some instances to mix elements collectively.
3. Top with ultimate bacon and inexperienced onions.
4. Serve with chips.

Nutrition facts: Calories: 323kcal, **Carbohydrates:** 5g, **Protein:** 18g, **Fat:** 24g, **Sugar:** 3g

BUFFALO CHICKEN DIP

prep times: 10min **cook times: 90**min **total times: 100**min , **serving: 6 -8**

Ingredients:

- 1 - (8-ounce) block reduced-fat cream cheese, roughly cut into 1-inch cubes
- 4 - ounces crumbled blue cheese
- 3 - cups diced or shredded cooked chicken
- 2 - cups shredded part-skim mozzarella cheese
- 1 - cup hot sauce
- 1 - cup plain Greek yogurt or sour cream
- ½ cup thinly-sliced green onions
- 1 - Tbsp ranch seasoning

Instructions:

1. Shower within the bowl of your moderate cooker with cooking splash.
2. Add all fixings to the bowl of the moderate cooker, and mix until joined.
3. Cook on high for 1.5 – 2 HRS, or until the cheeses are completely dissolved. Give the plunge a decent last mix; at that point move to a serving bowl and embellishment with additional blue cheddar and green onions whenever wanted. Present with chips or your ideal scoops.

Nutrition facts:

Calories 234, **fat** 17g, **carbohydrate** 2g, **Protein** 19g.

Puff Pastry Pizza Twists

Prep Time10min **Cook Time**15min **Total Time**25min, **serving: 27**

Ingredients:

- 2 - sheets puff pastry defrosted if frozen
- ¼ cup tomato sauce plus more for dipping
- ¾ cup mozzarella shredded low-moisture

- 1 egg yolk
- 1 teaspoon water
- ½ teaspoon dried oregano
- ¼ teaspoon garlic powder
- ¼ cup grated Parmesan cheese

Instructions :

1. Preheat broiler to 400°F and fix two heating sheets with material or softly oil.
2. On a gently floured surface, roll the 2 sheets of puff cake into smooth, equivalent square shapes.
3. Brush the tomato sauce over the highest point of one of the puffs baked good sheets, leaving a ½ inch outskirt around the edges. Sprinkle equally with the destroyed mozzarella. Top with the other sheet of puff baked well.
4. In a little bowl, beat together the egg yolk and water. Brush over the highest point of the puff baked well. Equally top with the oregano, garlic powder, and ground Parmesan cheddar.
5. Cut the sheet the long way into 9 equivalents long strips, at that point across twice to slice the strips into thirds to make 27 little sticks. Bend each stick tenderly while holding the two sheets together and place it on the readied heating sheet.
6. Heat in the preheated stove until puffed and brilliant, around 15-20min. Present with extra tomato sauce for plunging.

Nutrition facts: Calories 123, **fat** 6g, **carbohydrate** 15g, **Protein** 3g.

Ninja Foodi Meatballs

Prep Time/Total Time 45 min, **serving: 36**

Ingredients :

- 8 - medium fresh shiitake mushrooms minced
- 1 - medium shallot minced
- ¾ - cup minced sweet potato
- 2 - Tbsp minced cilantro
- 2 - pounds ground beef
- 1½ - Tbsp Red Boat fish sauce
- 2 - Tbsp tomato paste
- Mushroom Powder
- Freshly-ground black pepper
- 2 - Tbsp melted fat

Instructions:

1. Line two rimmed preparing sheets with material paper or foil, and preheat the stove to 375°F. Meanwhile, finely mince the mushrooms, shallot, yam, and cilantro.
2. In an enormous bowl, join the ground meat, fish sauce, tomato glue, and the minced veggies and herbs. Sprinkle on Magic Mushroom Powder and pepper. In case you're uncertain of how much flavoring to utilize, start with ½ teaspoons Magic Mushroom Powder and a couple of drudgeries of newly ground dark pepper. Altogether consolidate the fixings yet don't exhaust the meat.
3. To check if your flavoring is right, structure, and fry a min patty. Chow it down and alter the meatball blend for extra salt and pepper if necessary.
4. Scoop out uniform balls with medium dishes and turn out three dozen meatballs. Every meatball ought to be about 1½ crawl in breadth.
5. Gap the meatballs onto the two lined heating sheets. Prepare every plate of meatballs for 15 to 20min, pivoting the plate at the midpoint to guarantee in any event, cooking.
6. Plate and serve promptly, or store in a water/air proof holder in the ice chest for as long as three days. You can likewise freeze the concocted meatballs for a half year. Basically freeze them in a solitary layer and afterward place the strong spheres in a cooler pack or fixed compartment.

Nutrition:

Calories: 69 **Carbohydrates:** 1g **Protein:** 5g **Fat:** 5g **Fiber:** 1g

AVOCADO BRUSCHETTA WITH BALSAMIC REDUCTION

prep times: 10min **cook times: 20**min **total times: 30**min, **serving: 4**

Ingredients:
- 1 - baguette, thinly sliced
- ¼ cup olive oil, divided
- ½ cup balsamic vinegar
- 2 - Tbsp brown sugar, packed
- 2 - cups cherry tomatoes, halved
- 1 - avocado, halved, seeded, peeled and diced
- Kosher salt and freshly ground black pepper
- ¼ cup basil leaves, chiffonier

Instructions:
1. Set the heat level to 350 F. Line a getting ready sheet with cloth paper.
2. Spot loaf cuts onto the readied heating sheet. Shower with 2 Tbsp olive oil. Spot into broiler and heat for 8-10min, or until incredible earthy colored.
3. To make the balsamic lower, together with balsamic vinegar and earthy colored sugar to a bit pan over medium warm temperature. Bring to a slight bubble and reduce notably, round 6-8min; put in a secure spot and let cool.
4. In a substantial bowl, be a part of tomatoes, avocado, staying 2 Tbsp olive oil, salt, and pepper, to taste.
5. Top every roll cut with tomato blend, embellished with basil.
6. Serve fast, showered with balsamic lower.

Nutrition facts:
Calories 179, **fat** 6g, **carbohydrate** 12g, **Protein** 18g.

Bacon-Wrapped Figs With Blue Cheese And Bourbon Caramel

prep times: 15 min **cook times:** 10 min **total times:** 25min , **serving:** 16

Ingredients:

- 8 - slices thick-cut bacon, cut in half
- 8 - firm, ripe fresh figs, halved lengthwise
- 6 - ounces creamy blue cheese, crumbled
- ½ cup bourbon
- ¾ cup (6 ounces) unsalted butter
- ¾ lightly packed cup light brown sugar
- Flaky salt, such as Maldon, for sprinkling

Instructions:

1. Preheat the grill and set the broiler rack in top position. Line a rimmed heating sheet with aluminum foil.
2. In an enormous skillet over medium warmth, cook bacon until a large portion of the fat has rendered however the bacon is as yet malleable. Move the bacon to a paper towel-lined plate to assimilate overabundance oil. Put in a safe spot.
3. Utilizing a melon hotshot or little spoon, scoop out the focal point of each split fig. Fill each emptied fig half with blue cheddar.
4. Fold a half-piece of bacon over each filled fig half and secure with toothpicks. Spot, cut side up, on the readied heating sheet.
5. In a medium pan, cook whiskey over medium warmth until decreased significantly. Race in the spread and earthy colored sugar until margarine is softened and earthy colored sugar is broken up. Keep on cooking, whisking at times, until sauce is sufficiently thick to cover the rear of a spoon.
6. Utilizing a baked good brush, brush whiskey coat everywhere throughout the top side of every bacon-wrapped fig. Sear until the bacon has cooked, about 4min. Sprinkle daintily with coarse ocean salt, whenever wanted, and serve warm.

Nutrition facts: Calories 165, fat 11g, carbohydrate 11g, Protein 4g.

Vegetarian

Grilled Ratatouille Pasta Salad

ACTIVE TIME25min **total TIME40**min, **serving: 4**

Ingredients:
- 2 - medium zucchini (about 1½ lb.), halved lengthwise
- 1 - medium or 2 small eggplants (about 1 lb.), cut into 1" wedges
- ¾ cup extra-virgin olive oil, divided
- 2½ tsp. kosher salt, divided
- 1 tsp. freshly ground black pepper, divided
- 10 oz. penne or casarecce pasta
- 1 - large or 2 medium heirloom or beefsteak tomato (about 1 lb.), cut into 1" pieces
- 8 oz. Ciliegini (min fresh mozzarella balls), drained, halved
- 2 - Tbsp. white balsamic or white wine vinegar
- 1 - Tbsp. thyme leaves
- 1 - cup basil leaves

Instructions:
1. Set up a Ninja Foodi oven broil for medium warmth. Hurl zucchini, eggplant, and ¼ cup oil on a rimmed preparing sheet; season with 1 tsp. salt and½ tsp. pepper. Barbecue, turning frequently, until hot, delicate, and singed all more than, 8 to 12min. come back to the heating sheet and let cool.
2. Cook pasta as per bundle directions:
3. Cut Ninja Foodi oven-broiled vegetables into scaled-down pieces and move to an enormous bowl. Include tomato, cheddar, vinegar, thyme, and 1½ tsp. salt, ½ tsp. pepper, and½ cup oil and blend to consolidate. Channel pasta and promptly add to bowl with vegetables. Blend well to join, at that point top with basil.
4. Do Ahead: Vegetables can be Ninja Foodi oven-broiled 3 days ahead. Move (entire) to an impermeable holder and chill.

Nutrition facts: Calories 90, fat 3g, carbohydrate 16g, Protein 3g.

Grilled Whole Cauliflower with Miso Mayo

ACTIVE TIME25min **total TIME40**min, **serving: 4–6**

Ingredients:

- 1 - large head of cauliflower, leaves removed, stem trimmed
- ½ tsp. (or more) kosher salt
- 4 - Tbsp. unsalted butter
- ¼ cup vinegar-based hot sauce
- 1 - Tbsp. ketchup
- 1 - Tbsp. soy sauce
- ½ cup mayonnaise
- 2 - Tbsp. white miso
- 1 - Tbsp. fresh lemon juice
- ½ tsp. freshly ground black pepper
- 2 - scallions, thinly sliced

Instructions:

1. Set up a Ninja Foodi oven broil for medium-high warmth. Sprinkle cauliflower done with salt in a huge microwave-safe bowl. Spread with cling wrap, puncture plastic a couple of times with a blade to vent, and microwave on high until a paring blade effectively slides into the stem, about 5min. Let cool somewhat.

2. Warmth spread, hot sauce, ketchup, and soy sauce in a little pot on the Ninja Foodi oven broil, mixing at times until margarine is liquefied, about 2min. Brush cauliflower is done with sauce and barbecue, secured, 10min. Turn cauliflower over, brush with sauce, and Ninja Foodi oven broil, secured, 10min. Keep on barbecuing, brushing and turning each 10min and warming sauce varying until cauliflower is softly singed on all sides and fork-delicate, 25 to 30min. The sauce ought to be spent at this point, yet in the event that not, brushes any residual sauce over. Move cauliflower to a plate and let cool somewhat.

3. Whisk mayonnaise, miso, lemon squeeze, and pepper in a medium bowl until smooth. Spread on a plate. Set cauliflower on top and disperse scallions over.

Nutrition facts: Calories 130, fat 3g, carbohydrate 2g, Protein 3g.

Grilled Whole Eggplant with Harissa Vinaigrette

ACTIVE TIME15min **total TIME45**min, **serving: 4**

Ingredients:

- 1 - Large eggplant (about 1½ lb.)
- 1 - tsp. kosher salt, divided
- ¼ cup extra-virgin olive oil
- 1 - Tbsp. fresh lemon juice
- 1 - Tbsp. harissa paste
- 1 - Tbsp. honey
- ¼ cup chopped parsley
- 4 to 6 (1"-thick) slices crusty bread, toasted on grill if desired

Instructions:

1. Set up a charcoal fire in a fish fry. Let coals cool to medium warm temperature.
2. Ninja Foodi oven broil eggplant straightforwardly on coals, turning at instances, until the skin is darkened and substance has crumpled, 15 to 20min. Transfer to a wire rack set interior a rimmed heating sheet and allow cool truly.
3. Cautiously expel skin from the eggplant, leaving stem unblemished. Season on all aspects with½ tsp. Salt. Let sit at the rack until overabundance water is depleted, 20 to 30min.
4. Whisk oil, lemon juice, harissa, nectar, and ultimate ½ tsp. Salt in a touch bowl to sign up for.
5. Utilizing a paring blade, make a few cuts down the length of eggplant on each side. Move to a plate and pour dressing over. Top with parsley and gift with bread close by.
6. Do Ahead: Eggplant may be dressed eight HRS ahead. Let sit at room temperature up to four HRS. Chill, if status by longer and permit take a seat at room temperature 60min before serving.

Nutrition facts:

Calories 270, **fat** 17g, **carbohydrate** 21g, **Protein** 10g.

Grilled Greens and Cheese on Toast

ACTIVE TIME25min **total TIME25**min, **serving: 2**

Ingredients:

- 2 - Tbsp. extra-virgin olive oil
- 1 - large bunches Tuscan kale, stems removed
- ½ tsp. kosher salt, plus more
- ½ tsp. freshly ground black pepper
- 6 - oz. cherry tomatoes
- ½ lb. Halloumi cheese, sliced into½" planks
- 1 - lemon, halved crosswise
- 4 - thick slices country-style bread
- 1 - large garlic clove, peeled, halved

Instructions:

1. Set up a Ninja Foodi oven broil for medium-high warmth. Oil grind. Hurl kale with 2 Tbsp. oil, ½ tsp. salt, and½ tsp. pepper in a huge bowl; put in a safe spot.
2. String tomatoes onto sticks, at that point shower with oil; season daintily with salt.
3. Ninja Foodi oven broil tomato sticks, Halloumi, and lemon parts turning sticks and cheddar partially through, until scorched and mellowed, 6–8min. Move to a platter.
4. In the interim, shower bread with oil; season delicately with salt. Ninja Foodi oven broil until brilliant earthy colored and fresh, about 2min per side. Move to a platter. Rub one side of each cut with the divided garlic clove.
5. Barbecue kale, setting it transversely across grind so it doesn't fall through the holes and turning sporadically, until scorched in places and mellowed all through, 2 to 3min. Move to platter close by Halloumi, tomatoes, and bread.
6. Push tomatoes off sticks. Crush singed lemon parts over Halloumi, tomatoes, kale, and bread. Sprinkle with oil.

Nutrition facts: Calories 320, **fat** 9g, **carbohydrate** 39g, **Protein** 17g.

Charred Green Beans with Ricotta & Lemon

ACTIVE TIME 15min **total TIME** 15min, **serving: 4**

Ingredients:
- 1½ pounds green beans, trimmed
- 2 - cups whole-milk ricotta
- 3 - Tbsp extra-virgin olive oil, plus more for drizzling
- ¾ teaspoon kosher salt, plus more
- 1 - teaspoon finely grated lemon zest
- Freshly ground black pepper
- Lemon wedges (for serving)

Instructions:
1. Set up a Ninja Foodi oven broil for medium-excessive warm temperature. In the case of utilizing a barbeque, mastermind inexperienced beans in a Ninja Foodi oven broil bin and see on a hot fish fry. Spread and Ninja Foodi oven broil, turning once part of the way through till beans are delicately burned and fresh delicate, about 8min. On the off threat that making use of a Ninja Foodi oven broil container, cook green beans legitimately on the dish, hurling at instances, till delicately singed, approximately 10min.
2. In the interim, making use of an electric powered blender on medium-rapid, whip ricotta, 3 Tbsp. Oil and ¾ tsp. Salt in a sizeable bowl till clean and soft, approximately 2min.
3. Spread whipped ricotta on the serving platter and organize roasted green beans over. Pour oil and sprinkle with lemon get-up-and-go; season with salt and pepper. Then place with lemon wedges at a close range.

Nutrition facts:
Calories 160, **fat** 11g, **carbohydrate** 16g, **Protein** 4g.

Fish & Seafood

Ninja Foodi Cedar-Plank Salmon

ACTIVE TIMES: 30 min **TOTAL TIME2½ hr, serving: 6**

Ingredients:

- 2 - Tbsp grainy mustard
- 2 - Tbsp mild honey or pure maple syrup
- 1 - teaspoon minced rosemary
- 1 - Tbsp grated lemon zest
- 1 (2-pounds) salmon fillet with skin (1½ inches thick)

Instructions:

1. Splash cedar Ninja Foodi oven broiling board in water to cover 2 HRS, keeping it inundated.
2. Plan barbecue for direct-heat cooking over medium-hot charcoal. Open vents on the base and top of a charcoal Ninja Foodi oven broil.
3. Mix together mustard, nectar, rosemary, pizzazz, and ½ teaspoon every one of salt and pepper. Spread blends on the substance side of salmon and let remain at room temperature 15min.
4. Put salmon on board, skin side down. Barbecue, secured with a cover, until salmon is simply cooked through and edges are seared, 13 to 15min. Let salmon remain on board 5min before serving.

Nutrition facts:

Calories 240, **fat** 15g, **carbohydrate** 0g, **Protein** 23g.

Grilled Coconut Shrimp With Shishito Peppers

ACTIVE TIME25min **total TIME25**min, **serving: 4**

Ingredients: :

- 6 - garlic cloves, finely grated
- 1 - Tbsp. finely grated lime zest
- ¼ cup low-sodium
- ¼ cup grape seed or vegetable oil
- 1 lb. large shrimp, peeled, deveined
- ½ cup toasted unsweetened shredded coconut
- 8 - oz. shish to peppers
- ½ cup basil leaves
- ¼ cup fresh lime juice
- Flaky sea salt

Instructions:

1. Mix together garlic, lime get-up-and-go, soy sauce, and ¼ cup oil in a medium bowl. Add shrimp and hurl to cover. Include ½ cup coconut and hurl again to cover. Let sit while the Ninja Foodi oven broil warms, in any event, 5min and up to 30min.
2. Set up a Ninja Foodi oven broil for high warmth, delicately oil grind.
3. Cautiously organize shrimp in an even layer on the mesh. Ninja Foodi oven broil, cautiously turning part of the way through, until hazy and daintily singed, about 2min. A portion of the coconuts will tumble off all the while, and that is alright. Move to a serving platter.
4. Ninja Foodi oven broil peppers, turning every so often and being mindful so as not to let them fall through the mesh until delicately roasted all over about 6min. Move to platter with shrimp.
5. Top shrimp and peppers with basil, shower with a lime squeeze, and sprinkle with ocean salt and more coconut.

Nutrition facts:
Calories 82, **fat** 7g, **carbohydrate** 4g, **Protein** 2g.

Clams with Spicy Tomato Broth and Garlic Mayo

ACTIVE TIMES: 10 min **total times: 50** min, **serving: 4**

Ingredients:

- ½ lemon
- 5 - garlic cloves, 1 whole, 4 thinly sliced
- ½ cup mayonnaise
- Kosher salt
- ¼ cup plus 3 Tbsp. extra-virgin olive oil
- 2 - large shallots, thinly sliced
- 1 - red Chile (such as Holland or Fresno), thinly sliced, or½ tsp. crushed red pepper flakes
- 2 - Tbsp. tomato paste
- 2 - cups cherry tomatoes
- 1 - cup dry white wine
- 36 - littleneck clams, scrubbed
- 6 - Tbsp. unsalted butter, cut into pieces
- 3 - Tbsp. finely chopped chives
- 4 - thick slices country-style bread

Instructions:

1. Set up a Ninja Foodi oven broil for medium warmth. Finely grind the get-up-and-go from lemon half into a little bowl, at that point crush in the juice. Finely grind entire garlic clove into a bowl and blend in mayonnaise. Season garlic mayo with salt and put in a safe spot.
2. Spot a huge cast-iron skillet on the Ninja Foodi oven broil and warmth ¼ cup oil in a skillet. Include cut garlic, shallots, and Chile and cook, mixing regularly, until simply mollified, about 2min. Include tomato glue and cook, mixing frequently, until glue obscures somewhat, around 1 min. Include tomatoes and a touch of salt and cook, mixing every so often, until tomatoes mellow and discharge their juices, about 4min. Include wine and cook until it is nearly decreased considerably and no longer scents boozy about 3min.
3. Add shellfishes and margarine to the skillet and spread. Cook until shellfishes have opened, 6–10min, contingent upon the size of mollusks and warmth level. Expel skillet from Ninja Foodi oven broil; dispose of any mollusks that don't open. Sprinkle with chives.
4. In the interim, shower bread with the staying 3 Tbsp. oil and season softly with salt. Barbecue until brilliant earthy colored and fresh, about 3min per side.
5. Serve mollusks with toasted bread and saved garlic mayo.

Nutrition facts:
Calories 282, **fat** 10g, **carbohydrate** 0g, **Protein** 20g.

Grilled Swordfish with Tomatoes and Oregano

ACTIVE TIMES: 10 min **total times: 40** min, **serving: 4**

Ingredients:
- ½ cup plus 2 Tbsp. extra-virgin olive oil, plus more for grill
- 2 - Tbsp. pine nuts
- 2 - (12-oz.) swordfish steaks, about 1" thick
- Kosher salt, freshly ground pepper
- ¼ cup red wine vinegar
- 2 - Tbsp. drained capers, finely chopped
- 1 - Tbsp. finely chopped oregano, plus 2 sprigs for serving
- ½ tsp. honey
- 2 - large ripe heirloom tomatoes, halved, thickly sliced

Instructions:
1. Set up a Ninja Foodi oven broil for medium-high warmth; delicately oil grind. Toast pine nuts in a dry little skillet over medium warmth, shaking frequently, until brilliant, about 4min. Let cool and put in a safe spot for serving.
2. Pat swordfish dry and season did with salt and pepper. Spot on a rimmed preparing sheet and let sit at room temperature 15min.
3. Then, whisk vinegar, tricks, hacked oregano, nectar, and ½ cup oil in a little bowl to consolidate; put the marinade in a safe spot. Mastermind tomatoes on a rimmed platter, covering somewhat; put in a safe spot.
4. Rub swordfish done with the staying 2 Tbsp. oil and Ninja Foodi oven broil, undisturbed, until barbecue marks show up, about 4min. cautiously turn over and cook on the second side until fish is misty entirely through, about 4min. Move to saved platter with tomatoes and top with oregano branches. Season with increasingly salt and pepper. Pour held marinade over and let sit in any event 15min and as long as 60 minutes. To serve, disperse saved pine nuts over.

Nutrition facts:
Calories 210, **fat** 10g, **carbohydrate** 0g, **Protein** 30g.

Grilled Spiced Snapper with Mango and Red Onion Salad

ACTIVE TIMES: 10 min **total times: 30** min, **serving: 4**

Ingredients:

- 1 (5-lb.) or 2 (2½-lb.) head-on whole fish, cleaned
- Kosher salt
- 1/3 - cup chaat masala, vadouvan, or tandoori spice
- 1/3 - cup vegetable oil, plus more for grill
- 1 - ripe but firm mango, peeled, cut into irregular 1½" pieces
- 1 - small red onion, thinly sliced, rinsed
- 1 - bunch cilantro, coarsely chopped
- 3 - Tbsp. fresh lime juice
- Extra-virgin olive oil
- Lime wedges (for serving)

Instructions:

1. Spot fish on a cutting board and pat dry altogether with paper towels. With a sharp blade, make slices across on an askew along the body each 2" on the two sides, chopping right down to the bones. Season fish liberally all around with salt. Coat fish with flavor blend, pressing on more if necessary. Let sit at room temperature 20min.
2. In the interim, set up a Ninja Foodi oven broil for medium-high warmth. Clean and oil grind.
3. Shower the two sides of fish with staying 1/3 cup vegetable oil to cover. Ninja Foodi oven broil fish undisturbed, 10min. Lift up somewhat from one edge to check whether the skin is puffed and softly roasted and effectively discharges from the mesh. If not exactly prepared, take off alone for another min or somewhere in the vicinity and attempt once more. When it is prepared, delicately slide 2 huge metal spatulas underneath and turn over. Barbecue fish until the opposite side is daintily roasted and skin is puffed, 8–12min, contingent upon the size of the fish. Move to a platter.
4. Sling mango, onion, cilantro, lime juice, and a major spot of salt in a medium bowl. Sprinkle with a touch of olive oil and sling again to cover. Disperse mango plate of mixed greens over fish and present with lime wedges for pressing over.

Nutrition facts:
Calories 224, **fat** 9g, **carbohydrate** 17g, **Protein** 24g.

Grilled Shrimp, Zucchini, and Tomatoes with Feta

ACTIVE TIME15min **total TIME15**min, **serving: 2**

Ingredients:
- 1 - large garlic clove, finely grated
- 2 - Tsp finely chopped oregano
- ¾ teaspoon kosher salt
- ¼ teaspoon crushed red pepper flakes
- 2 - Tbsp olive oil, plus more for a grill basket
- 10 - jumbo shrimp (about 8 ounces), peeled, deveined, tails left on
- 1 - medium zucchini (about 8 ounces), sliced into ¼" rounds
- 1 - pint cherry tomatoes
- 2 - pita pockets
- 1/3 - cup crumbled feta (about 1.5 ounces)
- Special Equipment
- A flat grill basket (about 13½ x 8½")

Instructions:
1. Set up a Ninja Foodi oven broil for high warmth. Whisk garlic, oregano, salt, red pepper, and 2 Tbsp. oil in an enormous bowl. Include shrimp, zucchini, and tomatoes and hurl to cover.
2. Brush wires of Ninja Foodi oven broil container with oil, at that point, include shrimp blend. Mastermind in an even layer and close container. Spot barbecue container on Ninja Foodi oven broil and cook, turning regularly until shrimp are completely cooked through and zucchini and tomatoes are delicately singed about 6min.
3. In the meantime, barbecue pita just until warm and toasted.
4. Move shrimp blend to an enormous bowl and hurl until covered with tomato juices. Partition among plates and top with feta. Present with pita close by.

Nutrition facts: Calories 178, **fat** 3g, **carbohydrate** 12g, **Protein** 24g.

Grilled Salmon Steaks with Cilantro-Garlic Yogurt Sauce

ACTIVE TIMES: 10 min **total times: 30** min**, serving: 4**

Ingredients:

- Vegetable oil (for the grill)
- 2 - Serrano chiles
- 2 - garlic cloves
- 1 - cup cilantro leaves with tender stems
- ½ - cup plain whole-milk Greek yogurt
- 1 - Tbsp. extra-virgin olive oil
- 1 - tsp. honey
- 2 - (12-oz.) bone-in salmon steaks
- Kosher salt

Instructions:

1. Set up a Ninja Foodi oven broil for medium-high warmth; oil grind. Expel and dispose of seeds from 1 Chile. Purée the two chiles, garlic, cilantro, yogurt, oil, nectar, and ¼ cup water in a blender until smooth; season well with salt. Move half of sauce to a little bowl and put in a safe spot for serving.
2. Season salmon steaks daintily with salt. Barbecue, turning on more than one occasion until substance is beginning to turn misty, about 4min. Keep on Ninja Foodi oven broiling, turning regularly and seasoning with residual sauce, until misty completely through, about 4min longer. Present with held sauce nearby.

Nutrition facts: Calories 282, **fat** 15g, **carbohydrate** 0g, **Protein** 34g.

Garlicky Grilled Squid with Marinated Peppers

ACTIVE TIMES: 10 min **total times: 20** min, **serving: 4**

Ingredients:
- 1/3 - cup coarsely chopped blanched hazelnuts or almonds
- 2 - Tbsp. plus½ cup extra-virgin olive oil, divided
- Kosher salt
- 4 - large red bell peppers
- 2 - Tbsp. sherry vinegar or red wine vinegar
- 1 - tsp. hot smoked Spanish paprika
- 3 - garlic cloves, divided
- 1½ lb. cleaned squid, bodies and tentacles separated
- ½ - small red onion, very thinly sliced
- 1 - cup mint leaves, torn if large
- ½ lemon

Instructions:
1. Preheat stove to 350°F. Toast hazelnuts on a rimmed preparing sheet, hurling once, until brilliant earthy colored, 7–10min. Let cool, at that point pulverize nuts utilizing the side of a culinary expert's blade or coarsely cleave. Move to a little bowl. Blend in 2 Tbsp. oil and season with salt. Put in a safe spot.
2. Set up a Ninja Foodi oven broil for high warmth and spot a wire rack on one side, arranging it opposite to the barbecue grind. Spot chime peppers legitimately on the mesh and Ninja Foodi oven broil, turning at times, until roasted all finished and substance is delicate, 8–10min.
3. Move ringer peppers to a medium bowl and spread firmly with cling wrap. Let sit 10–20min. Take skins out from peppers and scoop out seeds; dispose of. Tear or cut peppers into big pieces and spot them in a perfect medium bowl. Include vinegar, paprika, and ¼ cup oil and finely grind 1 garlic clove into a bowl. Season with salt and hurl well to cover peppers.
4. Return Ninja Foodi oven broil to high warmth. Finely grind the staying 2 garlic cloves into a huge bowl; mix in remaining ¼ cup oil. Pat squid dry at that point add to oil blend; hurl well to cover. Working in clumps, Ninja Foodi oven broil squid on a wire rack on the barbecue until marks show up on bodies and limbs start too fresh around the edges, 45–60 seconds for each side. Move to a perfect huge bowl and season with salt.
5. Spot onion and mint in a little bowl. Finely grind the pizzazz from lemon half-finished; at that point crush in the juice. Season with salt and hurl to join. Partition marinated peppers and squid among plates. Spoon hazelnuts over and top with mint plate of mixed greens.

Nutrition facts: Calories 105, **fat** 1g, **carbohydrate** 12g, **Protein** 13g.

Grilled Turbot with Celery Leaf Salsa Verde

ACTIVE TIMES: 10 min **total times: 40** min **serving: 8**

Ingredients:
- 2 - whole turbot, heads and fins removed, split in half along the backbone
- 1¼ cups extra-virgin olive oil, divided
- Kosher salt
- 8 - sprigs rosemary, divided
- 1½ cups finely chopped parsley
- ½ cup finely chopped celery leaves
- 1 - garlic clove, finely grated
- ½ - lemon
- ½ tsp. Aleppo-style or other mild red pepper flakes
- Freshly ground black pepper
- Aioli or store-bought mayonnaise (for serving)

Instructions:
1. Set up a Ninja Foodi oven broil for medium-low backhanded warmth. Detach 4 huge sheets of foil. Rub fish with ½ cup oil (2 Tbsp. per piece) and season with salt. Working each in turn, place a filet in the focal point of a sheet of foil and top with 2 rosemary twigs. Crease in short sides of the foil over fish, at that point overlap in long sides and move edges together to seal.
2. Spot pockets on the cool side of the Ninja Foodi oven broil, spread barbecue, and cook fish, turning once, 20–25min. open a pocket to check fish. The substance ought to be somewhat murky and the tip of a blade should slide through without any problem. Barbecue somewhat more if necessary.
3. In the interim, consolidate parsley, celery leaves, and garlic in a medium bowl. Finely get-up-and-go the lemon into a bowl, at that point crush in the juice. Include red pepper drops and blend in remaining ¾ cup oil; season with salt and dark pepper. Let salsa Verde sits 10min for flavors to meet up.
4. Move fish to a platter and present with salsa Verde and aioli

Nutrition facts:
Calories 234, **fat** 10g, **carbohydrate** 0g, **Protein** 33g.

Grilled Clams With Herb Butter

ACTIVE TIMES: 10 min **total times: 30** min **serving: 6**

Ingredients:

- ½ cup (1 stick) unsalted butter, room temperature
- 1 - Tbsp chopped flat-leaf parsley
- 1 - Tbsp chopped fresh dill
- 1 - Tbsp chopped scallion
- 1 - Tbsp fresh lemon juice
- Kosher salt and freshly ground black pepper
- 24 - littleneck clams, scrubbed
- Lemon wedges

Instructions:

1. Blend the initial 5 fixings in a medium bowl until all-around mixed. Season herb margarine to taste with salt and pepper.
2. Manufacture a medium-hot fire in a charcoal Ninja Foodi oven broil, or warmth a gas barbecue to high. Spot mollusks on the barbecue rack and spread Ninja Foodi oven broil with cover. Ninja Foodi oven broil until shellfishes simply open, 6 to 8min. Use tongs to move to a platter, being mindful so as to keep however much squeeze in the shells as could reasonably be expected.
3. Speck mollusks with herb margarine; let remain until spread melts. Serve warm with lemon wedges close by for crushing over.

Nutrition facts: Calories 159, **fat** 12g, **carbohydrate** 13g, **Protein** 3g.

Poultry

Ninja Foodi BBQ Grilled Chicken

prep times: 5 min **total times:** 30 min, **serving: 4**

Ingredients:

- 2 c. barbecue sauce
- Juice of 1 lime
- 2 - tbsp. honey
- 1 - tbsp. hot sauce
- Kosher salt
- Freshly ground black pepper
- 1 lb. boneless skinless chicken breasts
- Vegetable oil, for grill

Instructions:

1. In an enormous bowl, whisk together grill sauce, lime juice, nectar, and hot sauce, and season with salt and pepper. Set aside ½ cup for seasoning.
2. Add chicken to a bowl and sling until covered.
3. Warmth Ninja Foodi oven broil to high. Oil meshes and Ninja Foodi oven broil chicken, seasoning with held marinade, until roasted, 8min per side for bosoms, and 10 to 12min per side for drumsticks.

Nutrition facts:

Calories 180, **fat** 6g, **carbohydrate** 6g, **Protein** 25g.

Ninja Foodi Crack BBQ Chicken

prep times: 15 min **total times: 2 HRS 30** min **serving: 8**

Ingredients:

- 1 - lb. boneless skinless chicken breasts
- 2 - c. water
- 2 - tbsp. kosher salt
- ¼ - c. brown sugar
- kosher salt
- Freshly ground black pepper
- 1 - c. barbecue sauce
- Juice of 2 limes
- 2 - cloves garlic, minced

Instructions:

1. Set the chook in a bib Ziploc sack and pound until ¼" thick. In a large mixing bowl, whisk collectively water, salt, and sugar until consolidated. Pour the saline answer into Ziploc and refrigerate in any occasion 15min, yet preferably 2 HRS.
2. Take the chook out from brackish water and put off fluid.
3. Warmth barbeque to medium. Include chook and season with salt and pepper, at that point Ninja Foodi oven broil 6min consistent with aspect.
4. In a medium bowl, whisk together grill sauce, lime juice, and garlic. Treat fowl, flipping sometimes, till caramelized and cooked through.

Nutrition facts:

Calories 122, **fat** 11g, **carbohydrate** 2g, **Protein** 20g.

Ninja Foodi Sticky Grilled Chicken

prep times: 10 min **total times: 2 HRS 35** min **serving: 4**

Ingredients:

- ½ c. low-sodium soy sauce
- ½ c. balsamic vinegar
- 3 tbsp. honey
- 2 - cloves garlic, minced
- 2 - green onions, thinly sliced
- 2½ lb. chicken drumsticks
- Vegetable oil, for grill
- 2 tbsp. sesame seeds, for garnish

Instructions:

1. In an enormous bowl, whisk together soy sauce, balsamic vinegar, nectar, garlic, and green onions. Put aside ¼ cup marinade.
2. Add chicken to an enormous resalable plastic pack and pour it in the outstanding marinade. Let marinate in the cooler at any rate 2 HRS or up to expedite.
3. At the point when prepared to barbecue, heat Ninja Foodi oven broils to high. Oil meshes and barbecue chicken, seasoning with the held marinade and turning each 3 to 4min, until sang and cooked through, 24 to 30min aggregate.
4. Embellishment with sesame seeds before serving.

Nutrition facts:

Calories 440, **fat** 8g, **carbohydrate** 51g, **Protein** 40g.

Ninja Foodi Grilled Chicken Breast

prep times: 15 min **total times:** 45 min **serving: 4**

Ingredients:

- ¼ c. balsamic vinegar
- 3 - tbsp. extra-virgin olive oil
- 2 - tbsp. brown sugar
- 3 - cloves garlic, minced
- 1 - tsp. dried thyme
- 1 - tsp. dried rosemary
- 4 - chicken breasts
- Kosher salt
- Freshly ground black pepper
- Freshly chopped parsley, for garnish

Instructions:

1. In a medium bowl, mix balsamic vinegar, olive oil, earthy colored sugar, garlic, and dried herbs altogether, and season liberally with salt and pepper. Hold ¼ cup.
2. Add bird to the bowl and hurl to sign up for. Let marinate in any occasion 20min and up to expedite.
3. Preheat Ninja Foodi oven broil to medium-high. Include hen and Ninja Foodi oven broil, treating with saved marinade, until cooked through, 6min according to facet.
4. Embellishment with parsley earlier than serving.

Nutrition facts:
Calories 208, **fat** 4g, **carbohydrate** 6g, **Protein** 0g.

Ninja Foodi Grilled Pineapple Chicken

prep times: 10 min **total times: 2 HRS 25** min **serving: 4**

Ingredients:

- 1 c. - unsweetened pineapple juice
- ¾ c. - ketchup
- ½ c. - low-sodium soy sauce
- ½ c. brown sugar
- 2 - cloves garlic, minced
- 1 - tbsp. freshly minced ginger
- 1 lb.- boneless skinless chicken breasts
- 1 - tsp. vegetable oil, plus more for the grill
- 1 - pineapple, sliced into rings & halved
- Thinly sliced green onions, for garnish

Instructions:

1. In an enormous bowl, whisk together pineapple juice, ketchup, soy sauce, earthy colored sugar, garlic, and ginger until joined.
2. Add chicken to an enormous plastic pack and pour in the marinade. Let marinate in the refrigerator in any event 2 HRS and up to expedite.
3. At the point when prepared to barbecue, heat Ninja Foodi oven broil to high. Oil meshes and Ninja Foodi oven broil chicken, seasoning with marinade, until scorched and cooked through, 8min per side.
4. Sling pineapple with oil and Ninja Foodi oven broil until burned, 2min per side.
5. Topping chicken and pineapple with green onions before serving.

Nutrition facts:

Calories 171, **fat** 1g, **carbohydrate** 12g, **Protein** 27g.

Ninja Foodi Grilled Chicken Wings

prep times: 10 min **total times: 35** min **serving: 4**

Ingredients:

FOR THE WINGS
- Zest of 1 lemon
- 2 - tsp. kosher salt
- 1 - tsp. smoked paprika
- 1 - tsp. garlic powder
- 1 - tsp. onion powder

- 1 - tsp. dried thyme
- ¼ tsp. cayenne
- 2 lb.- chicken wings
- Vegetable oil, for the grill

FOR THE SAUCE
- ½ c. mayonnaise
- Juice of 1 lemon
- 1 - tbsp. Dijon mustard
- 2 - tsp. horseradish

- 2 - tsp. freshly chopped chives
- 1 - tsp. hot sauce, such as Crystal

Instructions:
1. In a medium bowl, whisk together lemon get-up-and-go, salt, paprika, garlic powder, onion powder, thyme, and cayenne. Pat chicken wings dry and see in a big bowl. Add taste combination and sling to cover.
2. Warm Ninja Foodi oven broil or barbeque dish to medium warm temperature. Oil Ninja Foodi oven broil grates with vegetable oil. Include wings and cook, mixing on occasion, till the skin is fresh and meat is cooked via 15 to 20min.
3. In the period in-between, make the sauce: In a medium bowl, whisk collectively mayo, lemon juice, mustard, horseradish, chives, and hot sauce.
4. Serve wings hot with plunging sauce.

Nutrition facts: Calories 129, **fat** 7g, **carbohydrate** 5g, **Protein** 10g.

Ninja Foodi Sweet Chili-Lime Grilled Chicken

prep times: 10 min **total times: 2 HRS 25** min **serving: 4**

Ingredients:

- ¾ c. sweet chili sauce
- Juice of 2 limes
- 1/3 - c. low-sodium soy sauce
- 4 - boneless skinless chicken breasts
- Vegetable oil, for the grill
- Thinly sliced green onions, for garnish
- Lime wedges, for serving

Instructions:

1. In an enormous bowl, whisk together bean stew sauce, lime juice, and soy sauce. Put aside 1/4 cup marinade.
2. Add chicken to an enormous plastic sack and pour in the marinade. Let marinate in the cooler at any rate 2 HRS or up to expedite.
3. At the point when prepared to Ninja Foodi oven broil, heat barbecue to high. Oil meshes and Ninja Foodi oven broil chicken, treating with marinade until burned and cooked through, about 8min per side.
4. Season with held marinade and enhancement with green onions. Present with lime wedges.

Nutrition facts:

Calories 340, **fat** 7g, **carbohydrate** 41g, **Protein** 26g.

Honey Balsamic Grilled Chicken Thighs

prep times: 10 min **total times: 1 HOUR 25** min **serving: 4**

Ingredients:

- 8 - bone-in, skin-on chicken thighs
- Kosher salt
- Freshly ground black pepper
- 2 - tbsp. butter
- 2 - tbsp. balsamic vinegar
- 1/3 - c. honey
- 3 - cloves garlic, peeled and crushed
- Canola oil, for greasing
- Chopped chives, for garnish
- Chopped parsley, for garnish
- Lemon wedges, for garnish

Instructions:

1. Spot the chicken thighs on an enormous plate and sprinkle with salt and pepper on all sides. Work the flavoring into the chicken. Let sit, in the fridge, for in any event 60 minutes.
2. Then, make the coating: In a medium pot, soften the spread. Include the vinegar, nectar, and garlic and mix until the nectar has broken down. Season with salt and pepper. Set close to the barbecue.
3. Preheat barbecue to medium-high and clean and oil the meshes with canola oil. Include chicken skin-side-down and Ninja Foodi oven broil, flipping frequently and seasoning with sauce, until cooked through, 10min per side.
4. Present with lemon wedges and trimming with chives and parsley

Nutrition facts:
Calories 440, **fat** 24g, **carbohydrate** 35g, **Protein** 21g.

Ninja Foodi Italian Chicken Skewers

prep times: 15 min **total times: 25** min **serving: 8**

Ingredients:

- 1 lb. boneless skinless chicken breasts, cut into large cubes
- kosher salt
- Freshly ground black pepper
- 2 tbsp. tomato paste
- ¼ c. extra-virgin olive oil, plus more for drizzling
- 3 - garlic cloves, minced
- 1 - tbsp. chopped fresh Italian parsley, plus more leaves for garnish
- 8 - skewers, soaked in water for 20min
- 1 - baguette French bread, cut into cubes

Instructions:

1. Season chicken with salt and pepper. Make the marinade: consolidate tomato glue, olive oil, garlic cloves, and slashed parsley in a huge bowl. Add chicken and hurl to completely cover. Refrigerate 30min.
2. Preheat Ninja Foodi oven broil to medium-high. Stick chicken and bread. Shower with olive oil and season with salt and pepper.
3. Ninja Foodi oven broil, turning every so often until chicken is cooked through and bread marginally burned, about 10min. Embellishment with parsley.

Nutrition facts:

Calories 260, **fat** 8g, **carbohydrate** 7g, **Protein** 38g.

Ninja Foodi California Grilled Chicken

prep times: 20 min **total times: 40** min **serving: 4**

Ingredients:

-
- ¾ c. balsamic vinegar
- 1 - tsp. garlic powder
- 2 - tbsp. honey
- 2 - tbsp. extra-virgin olive oil
- 2 - tsp. Italian seasoning
- Kosher salt
- Freshly ground black pepper
- 4 - boneless skinless chicken breasts
- 4 - slices mozzarella
- 4 - slices avocado
- 4 - slices tomato
- 2 - tbsp. Freshly sliced basil, for garnish
- Balsamic glaze, for drizzling

Instructions:

1. In a little bowl, whisk together balsamic vinegar, garlic powder, nectar, oil, and Italian flavoring and season with salt and pepper. Pour over chicken and marinate 20min.
2. At the point when prepared to Ninja Foodi oven broil, heat barbecue to medium-high. Oil meshes and Ninja Foodi oven broil chicken until scorched and cooked through, 8min per side.
3. Top chicken with mozzarella, avocado, and tomato and spread barbecue to liquefy, 2min.
4. Enhancement with basil and shower with balsamic coating.

Nutrition facts:

Calories 468, **fat** 23g, **carbohydrate** 38g, **Protein** 29g.

Beef Pork, and Lamb

Tender Grilled Short Ribs Recipe

ACTIVE TIMES: 15min **total times:** 30min **serving: 4**

Ingredients:
- 2 - pounds boneless short ribs
- Kosher salt and freshly ground black pepper

Instructions:
1. In the occasion that utilizing boneless short ribs, cut into four 8 ounce parcels, around 2 inches huge and six inches in duration every. In the occasion that making use of English-reduce off ribs, utilize a pointy blade to expel meat from bones. Spare bones for some other utilization.
2. Light one smokestack brimming with charcoal. At the factor whilst all the charcoal is lit and secured with darkish particles, spill out and mastermind the coals on one facet of the charcoal mesh. Set cooking grate set up, spread barbecue, and permit to preheat for 5min. On the opposite hand, set a huge part of the burners on a fuel Ninja Foodi oven broil to the most noteworthy warmth putting, spread, and preheat for 10min. Clean and oil the Ninja Foodi oven broiling grate.
3. Season quick ribs generously with salt and pepper and notice straightforwardly over coals. Cook, turning as often as viable until roasted on all facets and check thermometer embedded into the thickest piece of steak register 125°F, eight to 10min aggregate. Move to a slicing board, tent with foil, and permit rest for 5min.
4. Meagerly cut quick ribs opposite to what might be anticipated and serve right away.

Nutrition facts:
Calories 294, **fat** 22g, **carbohydrate** 0g, **Protein** 11g.

Crying Tiger (Grilled Steak With Dry Chili Dipping Sauce)

ACTIVE TIMES: 30min **total times:** 30min **serving:** 4

Ingredients:

- 4 - rib-eye or New York strip steaks, about 1½-inches thick
- 2 - Tbsp dark soy sauce
- 1 - Tbsp oyster sauce
- 1 - Tbsp light or dark brown sugar
- 1 - Tbsp plain vegetable oil
- 2 - plum tomatoes

Instructions:

1. Combine the soy sauce, clam sauce, earthy colored sugar, and vegetable oil in a medium blending bowl. Coat the steaks with the soy sauce blend and let them marinate while you chip away at the plunging sauce.
2. Strip and deseed the tomatoes. Cleave the mash finely, and add it to arranged dried bean stew plunging sauce (Jaew); put in a safe spot.
3. Light one stack brimming with charcoal. At the point when all the charcoal is lit and secured with dim debris, spill out and spread the coals equally over the whole surface of coal grind. Set cooking grate set up, spread Ninja Foodi oven broil, and permit to preheat for 5min. On the other hand, set all the burners on a gas Ninja Foodi oven broil to high warmth. Clean and oil the barbecuing grate.
4. Ninja Foodi oven broil the steaks, turning every now and again until the ideal doneness is reached. Expel from Ninja Foodi oven broil and let rest for 5min.
5. Cut the steaks into ¼-inch cuts and present with the plunging sauce. Warm clingy rice as an afterthought is enthusiastically suggested

Nutrition facts:

Calories 288, **fat** 11g, **carbohydrate** 3g, **Protein** 36g.

Memphis-Style Dry Ribs

ACTIVE TIMES: 1½ to 2 HRS total times: 1½ to 2 HRS, serving: 4

Ingredients:

For the Dry Rub:

-
- ½ cup paprika
- 1/3 - cup dark brown sugar
- ¼ - cup kosher salt
- 2 - Tbsp granulated garlic
- 1 - Tbsp celery salt
- 1 - Tbsp chili powder
- 1 - Tbsp freshly ground black pepper

- 2 - Tsp onion powder
- 2 - Tsp dried thyme
- 2 - Tsp dried oregano
- 2 - Tsp mustard powder
- 1 - teaspoon celery seed
- ½ - teaspoon cayenne pepper

For the Mop:

-
- ½ cup distilled white vinegar
- ½ cup water

- ¼ cup dry rub
- 2 - racks baby back ribs

Instructions:

1. For the dry rub: Mix together paprika, dim earthy colored sugar, genuine salt, granulated garlic, celery salt, bean stew powder, dark pepper, onion powder, dried thyme, dried oregano, mustard powder, and celery seed in a little bowl.
2. To make the mop: Whisk together vinegar, water, and dry focus on a little bowl. Put in a safe spot.
3. Fire up smoker or barbecue to 325°F. On the off chance that utilizing a vertical water smoker, for example, the Weber Smokey Mountain, place ribs on top rack with water skillet evacuated. On the off chance that utilizing a Ninja Foodi oven broil or balance smoker, place ribs over backhanded warmth. Cook until ribs have a slight twist when lifted from one end, about 1½ HRS for child's backs and 2 HRS for St. Louis-cut ribs, brushing generously with the mop each 15-20min.
4. Move ribs to cut board and brush with a mop. Generously cover ribs with rub and let rest for 5min. Cut ribs and serve right away.

Nutrition facts: Calories 290, **fat** 23g, **carbohydrate** 4g, **Protein** 15g.

Ninja Foodi Grilled Steaks

ACTIVE TIMES: 15min total times: 1½ HRS, or up to 4 days, serving: 2 to 3

Ingredients:

- 2 - large ribeye or
- Kosher salt and freshly ground black pepper

Instructions:

1. Season steaks liberally with salt. Set on a plate and let relaxation for at the least 40min or up to four days. If resting longer than 40min, transfer to a twine rack set in a rimmed baking sheet and refrigerate, uncovered, until equipped to prepare dinner.

2. Light one chimney complete of charcoal. When all charcoal is lit and included with gray ash, pour out and set up coals on one facet of the charcoal grate. Set cooking grate in location, cowl grill, and permit to preheat for 5min. Clean and oil grilling grate. Season steak with pepper and area at the cooler side of the grill. Cover and prepare dinner, with all vents open, flipping and taking temperature every few min until steaks sign in 105°F (41°C) for medium-uncommon or one hundred 15°F (46°C) for medium on an immediate-read thermometer, 10 to 15min total.

3. Transfer steaks to the recent aspect of grill and prepare dinner, flipping often till a deep char has developed an inner temperature registers a hundred 25°F (fifty two°C) for medium-rare or 135°F (fifty seven°C) for medium, about 2min overall. Transfer steaks to a reducing board and allow to relaxation for at the least 5min and up to ten. Carve and serve straight away.

Nutrition facts: Calories 212, **fat** 10g, **carbohydrate** 0g, **Protein** 38g.

Grilled Italian-Style Meatballs With Pecorino and Parmesan

ACTIVE TIMES: 30min total times: 30min serving: 4 to 6

Ingredients:

- 1 - pound ground chuck
- ½ pound ground pork
- ¾ cup fresh bread crumbs
- 2 - large eggs, lightly beaten
- 1/3- cup grated Parmesan
- 1/3 - cup grated Pecorino Romano
- 2 - cloves garlic, minced
- 2 - Tbsp finely chopped fresh parsley
- ¼ teaspoon red pepper flakes
- Kosher salt
- Freshly ground black pepper
- Olive oil
- Marinara sauce, for dipping

Instructions:

1. In a huge bowl, mix together chuck, red meat, bread crumbs, eggs, Parmesan, Pecorino, garlic, parsley, and red pepper flakes until very well mixed. Roll out meat mixture into balls 1½ inches in diameter. Season meatballs all over liberally with salt and pepper.
2. Light one chimney complete of charcoal. When all of the charcoal is lit and included with gray ash, pour out and unfold the coals flippantly over the complete floor of coal grate. Set cooking grates in location, cowl grill, and allow preheating for 5min. Clean and oil the grilling grate. Brush meatballs with olive oil and vicinity on grill and cook dinner till well browned all over and cooked via, approximately 8min general, 2min according to side.
3. Remove meatballs to a platter and allow rest for 5min. Serve with marinara sauce.

Nutrition facts:

Calories 240, **fat** 17g, **carbohydrate** 7g, **Protein** 14g.

Ninja Foodi Juicy Grilled Pork Chops

ACTIVE TIMES: 30min **total times: 1 hour 30**min **serving: 4**

Ingredients:

- 4 (1½-inch-thick) center-cut pork rib chops, about 8 ounces (225g) each
- Kosher salt
- Freshly ground black pepper

Instructions:

1. Sprinkle red meat chops all over with salt, location on a cord rack set over a rimmed baking sheet, and refrigerate for at the least 1 hour and up to 24 HRS.
2. Remove beef chops from the refrigerator and season heavily with pepper. Lightly season with additional salt if important.
3. Light 1 chimney complete of charcoal. When all charcoal is lit and blanketed with grey ash, pour out and set up coals on one side of the charcoal grate. Set cooking grates in area, cover grill, and allow preheating for 5min. Clean and oil grilling grate. Place beef chops over the new aspect of the grill and cook till well browned, 3 to 5min in step with facet.
4. Move beef chops to chill side of the grill, situated with bones going through the fireplace. Cover and cook till meat registers one hundred thirty five°F (57°C) on an instantaneous-study thermometer whilst inserted into the thickest part of the chop. Remove pork from grill, allow relaxation for 10min, and then serve.

Nutrition facts:

Calories 290, **fat** 11g, **carbohydrate** 12g, **Protein** 34g.

Ninja Foodi Kansas City-Style Barbecue Ribs

ACTIVE TIMES: 1½ HRS total times: 6 to 7 HRS serving: 4

Ingredients:

For the rub:
- 1/3 - cup packed dark brown sugar
- ¼ - cup paprika
- 2 - Tbsp white sugar
- 2 - Tbsp celery salt
- 2 - Tbsp kosher salt
- 1 - Tbsp granulated onion
- 1 - Tbsp granulated garlic
- 1 - Tbsp chili powder
- 1 teaspoon ground white pepper
- 1 teaspoon ground black pepper
- For the Ribs:
- 2 racks pork ribs, baby backs or spare ribs
- 4 to 6 fist-size chunks of medium smoking wood, such as oak or hickory
- 1 recipe Kansas City-style barbecue sauce

Instructions:

1. Combine the earthy colored sugar, paprika, white sugar, celery salt, legitimate salt, granulated onion, granulated garlic, bean stew powder, white pepper, and dark pepper in a little bowl to make the rub.
2. Take the layer out from the rear of the rack, and trim the ribs of overabundance fat. Rub each rack generously with the rub. Enclose ribs by foil or spot in a huge holder and store in the fridge short-term.
3. Take the ribs out from the cooler while setting up the smoker or Ninja Foodi oven broil. Fire up smoker or Ninja Foodi oven broil to 225°F, including lumps of smoking wood pieces when at temperature. At the point when the wood is touched off and delivering smoke, place the ribs in the smoker or Ninja Foodi oven broil, meat side up, and smoke until the ribs have a slight twist when lifted from one end, around 4-5 HRS for infant backs or 5-6 HRS for saving ribs.
4. In the last½ hour of cooking, season the highest point of each rack with grill sauce and keep smoking. Take out from the smoker, cut, and serve.

Nutrition facts:
Calories 260, **fat** 17g, **carbohydrate** 6g, **Protein** 19g.

Ninja Foodi Competition Barbecue Pork Shoulder

ACTIVE TIMES: 1-hour total times: 10 to 14 HRS serving: 12-16

Ingredients:

For the Braise:
- ¾ cup apple juice
- ¼ cup cider vinegar
- ¼ cup brown sugar
- ¼ cup your favorite barbecue sauce

- 2 - Tbsp Worcestershire sauce
- 2 - Tbsp agave syrup
- 2 - Tbsp jalapeño jelly

For the Injection
- ½ cup apple juice
- ¼ cup brown sugar
- 3 - Tbsp cider vinegar
- 3 - Tbsp water
- 2 - Tbsp Worcestershire sauce

- 2 - Tbsp Kosher salt
- 1 - Boston pork butt (about 8 pounds)
- ¾ cup barbecue rub
- 2-3 fist-sized chunks of medium smoking wood, like oak or hickory

Instructions:

1. In a medium bowl, whisk collectively squeezed apple, vinegar, earthy colored sugar, grill sauce, Worcestershire sauce, agave, and jalapeño jam. Spread and positioned apart until organized to make use of.
2. To make the infusion: In a medium bowl, whisk together squeezed apple, earthy colored sugar, vinegar, water, Worcestershire sauce, and salt. Utilizing an infusion syringe, infuse the beef at 1-inch spans, utilizing the complete infusion association. Pat beef dry with paper towels.
3. Equally, cowl beef shoulder with grill rub everywhere.
4. Fire up smoker or Ninja Foodi oven broil to 225°F, along with lumps of smoking timber while at temperature. At the point whilst the timber is touched off and turning in smoke, place red meat imposes upon smoker or barbeque and smoke until the outside has grown to become profound mahogany shading, 5 to 7 HRS. Spot red meat button a bit of extra-big full-size aluminum foil with aspects collapsed upwards. Pour 1 cup of the braise over red meat butt. Save the last braise. Seal foil round pork, wrapping with more pieces various, and vicinity again in the smoker. Keep on cooking until inner temperature registers 198°F on a moment examine thermometer.
5. Take the beef out from smoker, open foil, and let vent for 15 to 30min. Maneuver beef into portions and see in a medium dish, preserving braise and casting off the bone. Pour held braise over arranged red meat and blend to absolutely disperse braise. Add extra braise to flavor. Serve proper away.

Nutrition facts:
Calories 300, **fat** 9g, **carbohydrate** 47g, **Protein** 8g.

Ninja Foodi Porterhouse Steaks

ACTIVE TIMES: 30min **total times: 3 HRS serving: 4**

Ingredients:
- 2 - whole porterhouse steaks, at least 1½ inches
- Kosher salt and freshly ground black pepper
- 8 chunks hickory or mesquite hardwood

Instructions:

1. Season steaks softly with salt and pepper on all surfaces, including edges. Stack steaks on a wood cutting board, at that point, embed up to four metallic sticks via the two steaks to ensure about them. Turn them on their facets, and spread them out on the sticks. They must stay on their edges without falling.
2. Light 8 coals utilizing a smokestack starter. The spot right on one edge of the coal grind in a charcoal Ninja Foodi oven broil. Then again, set one lot of burners on a gasoline barbecue to low. Spot 2 wood pieces on coals encompass the cooking mesh and spot steaks on the cooking grate with tenderloins confronting upwards and bones pointing toward the coals.
3. Spread Ninja Foodi oven broil and set-top and base vents to ¾ close. Position top vents over steaks. Cook, signifying 8 additional coals and final wood lumps to maintain the temperature below the Ninja Foodi oven broil at around a hundred seventy-five to two hundred°F. Screen the inner temperature of the steaks continuously and cook until steaks register a hundred and ten to one hundred fifteen°F for medium-uncommon or a hundred and twenty°F for medium, 1½ to 2 HRS. Expel steaks from Ninja Foodi oven broil and put a part on a reducing board.
4. Light one smokestack brimming with charcoal. At the point, while all of the charcoal is lit and secured with dark debris, spill out and mastermind the coals on one facet of the charcoal mesh. Set cooking grate installation, spread Ninja Foodi oven broil, and permit to preheat for 5min. On the alternative hand, set a huge part of the burners on a fuel Ninja Foodi oven broil to the most noteworthy warm temperature setting, unfold, and preheat for 10min. Clean and oil the Ninja Foodi oven broiling grate.
5. Spot steaks straightforwardly over the recent aspect of the Ninja Foodi oven broil. Spread and cook dinner for forty-five seconds. Flip steaks, spread, and cook dinner for forty-five seconds longer. Evacuate to a reducing board, cut, and serve.

Nutrition facts: Calories 418, **fat** 32g, **carbohydrate** 3g, **Protein** 31g.

Ninja Foodi Barbecue Short Ribs

ACTIVE TIMES: 30min **total times: 5 HRS serving: 6-8**

Ingredients:

For the rub
- 3 Tbsp Kosher salt
- 2 - Tbsp black pepper
- 2 - Tbsp white pepper
- 1 - Tbsp paprika
- 2 - teaspoon garlic powder
- 8 - full short ribs, cut into individual ribs
- 1 - cup apple juice in a spray bottle
- 3 to 4 - chunks of medium smoking wood,

Instructions:

1. In a little bowl join dark pepper, white pepper, salt, paprika, and garlic powder to make the rub. Season ribs all over generously with the rub.
2. Fire up smoker or barbecue to 225°F, including pieces of smoking wood lumps when at temperature. At the point when the wood is touched off and creating smoke, place the ribs in the smoker or Ninja Foodi oven broil, meat side up, and smoke until ribs arrive at 180 degrees on a moment read thermometer embedded into the center of the meat, around 4 to 5 HRS. Shower ribs with squeezed apple consistently during cooking.
3. Take ribs out from the smoker, let rest for 10min, at that point serve.

Nutrition facts: Calories 249, **fat** 22g, **carbohydrate** 0g, **Protein** 11g.

Ninja Foodi Spice-Rubbed Grilled Skirt Steak

ACTIVE TIMES: 25min **total times: 2 HRS 25**min **serving: 12**

Ingredients:
- 2 - Tbsp cu min
- 2 - Tbsp ancho chili powder
- 2 - Tbsp paprika
- 1 - Tbsp salt
- 1 - Tbsp black pepper
- 1 - Tbsp cinnamon
- 8 - garlic cloves, minced
- ½ - cup olive oil
- 6 pounds skirt steak

Instructions:
1. In a touch bowl, crush together garlic and salt with the rear of a fork. Blend inside the flavors. Pour in olive oil and mix until thick glue structures.
2. Marinade: Rub the glue over all sides of steak. Spread steak and allow marinate within the cooler for 2 to12 HRS.
3. Ninja Foodi oven broil: Follow Josh Bousel's guidelines for wonderful barbecued skirt steak: Ignite a large fireplace brimming with coals and hold up till they are shrouded in dark debris. Spread equitably over½ of the mesh, leaving the alternative half unfilled. Set up the cooking mesh, spread, and allow the Ninja Foodi oven broil to preheat for 5min. Scratch cooking grates spotless, at that point area flank steak over the hot aspect of the Ninja Foodi oven broil. Prepare dinner until all-around scorched, approximately 3min.
4. Flip steak and preserve on cooking until the subsequent aspect is all around singed, about 3min longer. Move steak to the cooler facet of the barbeque, spread, and cook dinner until the focal point of the steak registers a hundred twenty five°F on a moment read thermometer for medium-uncommon or one hundred thirty five° for medium, about 5min longer. Move to a slicing board, tent with foil, and permit steak to rest for at any charge 5min.
5. To serve, cut steak over the grain in½ inch strips.

Nutrition facts:
Calories 339, **fat** 25g, **carbohydrate** 3g, **Protein** 24g.

Competition-Style Barbecue Ribs Recipe

ACTIVE TIMES: 2 HRS total times: 6 HRS serving: 4

Ingredients:
- 2 - racks St. Louis-cut pork ribs
- ½ - cup yellow mustard
- 1 - cup your favorite barbecue rub
- 2 - cups apple juice, divided, 1 cup placed in a squirt bottle
- 2 to 3 fist size chunks of light smoking wood, such as cherry or apple
- 1 - cup your favorite barbecue sauce
- ½ cup agave syrup (optional)
- ½ cup dark brown sugar (optional)

Instructions:
1. Take the movie out from the rear of each rack, and trim the ribs of overabundance fat. Brush meat aspect of every rack with yellow mustard; at that point rub generously with grill rub on the 2 aspects.
2. Fire up smoker or barbecue to 225°F, consisting of pieces of smoking wood while at temperature. At the factor while the wood is lighted and delivering smoke, vicinity the ribs within the smoker or Ninja Foodi oven broil, meat facet up. Smoke till ribs obscure to profound mahogany, round 3 HRS, clouding with a squeezed apple in a spurt bottle every hour.
3. Wrap every rack, meat side up, in greater-large hardcore aluminum foil, leaving an opening toward one side of the foil. Pour ½ cup of squeezed apple in every foil percent through the hole, seal and notice again on smoker or Ninja Foodi oven broil for 60 minutes.
4. Take out ribs from foil and spot ribs back in the smoker and maintain on cooking until ribs have a mild twist whilst lifted from one give up, 1 to 2 HRS increasingly more, spurting with squeezed apple continually. Take ribs out from smoker or Ninja Foodi oven broil, envelope by using foil, and a gap in a vacant cooler to keep heat whilst putting in place the barbeque.
5. Light one smokestack loaded with charcoal. At the point when all charcoal is lit and secured with dim debris, spill out and unfold the coals equally over the entire surface of coal grind. Set cooking grate set up, spread Ninja Foodi oven broil, and permit to preheat for 5min. Clean and oil the Ninja Foodi oven broiling grate. Take the racks out from foil and brush with grill sauce. Spot ribs face down over warm fire and cook till sauce caramelizes 2 to 5min. Take racks out from the barbecue.
6. For extra candy and sleek ribs: Tear off two extra big sheets of aluminum foil longer than each rack. In a rectangular form, the inexact length of every rack of ribs unfold ¼ cup of agave syrup and sprinkle ¼ cup earthy colored sugar on agave on each little bit of foil. Spot ribs, meat facet down, on agave and sugar, and wrap foil shut round ribs. Spot ribs returned at the smoker for 15min. Take ribs out from smoker and foil, at that point reduce and serve.

Nutrition facts: Calories 387, **fat** 25g, **carbohydrate** 13g, **Protein** 27g.

Ninja Foodi Rotisserie Porchetta

ACTIVE TIMES: 1½ hour total times: 6 HRS serving: 10

Ingredients:

For the Brine:
- 2 - quarts cold water
- 1/3 - cup salt
- ¼ - cup white sugar
- 1 - whole pork loin, trimmed of silver skin and excess fat

For the Rub:
- 1 - Tbsp whole black peppercorns
- 1 - Tbsp fennel seed
- 2 - Tbsp finely chopped fresh sage
- 1 - Tbsp finely chopped fresh rosemary
- 1 - Tbsp freshly minced garlic
- 2 - Tsp finely chopped fresh thyme
- 2 - Tsp crushed red pepper
- 1 - teaspoon lemon zest
- 1 - whole boneless pork belly

Instructions:

1. To make the saline solution: In a huge bowl, whisk together water, salt, and sugar until solids are broken down. Lower pork midsection in saline solution. A spot in cooler and brackish water for 2 HRS.
2. To make the rub: Place peppercorns and fennel seed in a cast-iron skillet over medium-high warmth; toast flavors until fragrant, about 2min. Move to a zest processor and procedure until coarsely ground. Move flavor blend to a little bowl and blend in sage, rosemary, garlic, thyme, squashed red pepper, and lemon get-up-and-go. Put in a safe spot.
3. Lay pork midsection, skin side down, on an enormous cutting board. Score tissue with a sharp blade at an edge about each inch. Rehash the other way to make a precious stone example. Season pork tummy generously with salt. Sprinkle rub equally across pork stomach, utilizing hands to pat rub into meat and cut cleft.
4. Take out pork flank from brackish water; pat dry with paper towels. A spot in the focal point of pork paunch. Move pork paunch around pork flank so it completely encases midsection. Tie move close with butcher twine about each inch.
5. Light one fireplace loaded with charcoal. At the point when all the charcoal is lit and secured with dim debris, spill out and orchestrate the coals on either side of the charcoal mesh and spot a foil skillet between the two heaps of coals. Spread barbecue and permit to preheat for 5min. Run spit of the rotisserie through the center of pork roll and secure closures with rotisserie forks. Spot on the rotisserie, spread, and cook at medium warmth until the skin has obscured and crisped and pork registers 155ºF when a moment read thermometer is embedded into the thickest piece of the meat, around 3 HRS, renewing coals to keep up temperature varying. Take out from the barbecue and let rest for 10min. Take it out spit, cut, and serve.

Nutrition facts: Calories 224, **fat** 16g, **carbohydrate** 1g, **Protein** 19g.

Vietnamese Grilled Lemongrass Pork Chops

ACTIVE TIMES: 30min **total times: 1 hour serving: 6**

Ingredients:

For the Pork:
- 2 - Tsp whole white peppercorns, or 1½ Tsp ground white pepper (4g)
- Pinch kosher salt
- 3 - stalks lemongrass, bottom 4 to 5 inches only, outer leaves discarded, tender core thinly sliced
- 1 - small shallot, roughly chopped
- 4 - medium cloves garlic, roughly chopped
- 1/3 - cup palm sugar
- ¼ - cup (60ml) fish sauce
- 2 - Tbsp (30ml) vegetable oil
- 1½ pounds (680g) thin-cut pork chops, preferably blade end, with plenty of fat and marbling

For the Sauce:
- 1 - recipe basic Nuoc Cham
- ¼ cup (30g) very thinly julienned or grated carrot
- ¼ cup (30g) very thinly julienned or grated daikon radish
- Pinch crushed red pepper flakes

Instructions:
1. For the Pork: If utilizing entire white peppercorns, pound with salt in a mortar and pestle until generally squashed. Include salt, lemongrass, shallot, garlic, palm sugar, and pre-ground white pepper to mortar and smash to a harsh glue. You can keep squashing by hand now or move to a food processor to complete the activity.
2. Move marinade to a bowl and rush in fish sauce and vegetable oil. Include pork slashes, going them to cover all surfaces. Move pork to a gallon-size zipper-lock pack, press out the air, and seal sack. Marinate at room temperature, turning pork a few times, for at any rate 30min or up to 3 HRS. On the other hand, move to cooler and marinate, turning on more than one occasion, for up to 12 HRS before continuing.
3. For the Sauce: Prepare Nuoc Cham as per the formula, at that point add carrot and daikon to a similar bowl, if utilizing. Add stew chips to taste, if utilizing. The additional sauce can be put away in a sealed shut holder in the cooler for as long as a month.
4. Light one smokestack brimming with charcoal. At the point when all charcoal is lit and secured with dim debris, spill out and orchestrate coals on one side of the charcoal mesh. Set cooking grate set up, spread barbecue, and permit to preheat for 5min. On the other hand, set a large portion of the burners on a gas barbecue to the most noteworthy warmth setting, spread, and preheat for 10min. Clean and oil Ninja Foodi oven broiling grate. Ninja Foodi oven broil pork slashes legitimately over high warmth, turning habitually and moving to the cooler side of barbecue if there are unnecessary flare-ups until pork is burned and simply cooked through 4 to 6min aggregate. Move to a serving platter and serve quickly with steamed white rice, cut cucumber, and sauce.

Nutrition facts: Calories 425, **fat** 23g, **carbohydrate** 22g, **Protein** 32g.

Pork Belly Marinated in Char Siu Sauce

ACTIVE TIMES: 1-hour total times: 10-16 HRS serving: 8

Ingredients:

-
- ½ cup char siu sauce
- ½ cup pineapple juice
- 5 - cloves garlic, finely minced
- 1 - Tbsp Kosher salt
- 1 - teaspoon freshly ground black pepper
- 4lbs pork belly, skin on
- 4 to 6 - chunks apple wood

Instructions:

1. In a medium bowl, combine roast siu sauce, pineapple juice, garlic, salt, and dark pepper.
2. Score the skin of the pork askew every 2-inches; rehash the other way, making a jewel design. Spot pork in a huge resalable plastic pack and pour in the marinade. Seal and hurl to uniformly cover. Marinate in the fridge for at any rate 4 HRS to expedite.
3. Take out the pork stomach and permit it to come to room temperature while setting up the smoker or Ninja Foodi oven broil. Fire up smoker or barbecue to 225°F for aberrant warmth, including lumps of apple wood when at temperature. At the point when the wood is touched off and creating smoke, place the pork in the smoker or Ninja Foodi oven broil, skin side up, and smoke until pork registers 160 degrees on a moment read thermometer embedded into the focal point of the gut, around 4 to 5 HRS.
4. Spot pork tummy on a medium-hot Ninja Foodi oven broil, skin side down, or in a grill, skin side up, and cook until skin is fresh. Evacuate to a cutting board, let rest for 10 to 15min, at that point cut and serve.

Nutrition facts:

Calories 234, **fat** 5g, **carbohydrate** 23g, **Protein** 22g.

Desserts

Ninja Foodi Grilled Donut Ice Cream Sandwich

prep times: 10 min **total times: 15** min **serving: 4**

Ingredients:

- 4 - glazed donuts, cut in half
- 8 - scoops vanilla ice cream
- Chocolate syrup, for drizzling
- whipped cream
- 4 - maraschino cherries

Instructions:

1. Preheat barbecue or Ninja Foodi oven broil skillet to high. Barbecue doughnut parts, coated side down, until burned, around 1 min. Put aside to cool.
2. Spot 2 scoops of vanilla dessert in the middle of every doughnut sandwich and press down.
3. Top each with a shower of chocolate syrup, whipped cream, and obviously, a wonderful finish!

Nutrition facts:

Calories 230, **fat** 9g, **carbohydrate** 34g, **Protein** 3g.

Foil Pack Chocolate Marshmallow Banana

total times: 10 min, **serving: 1**

Ingredients:

- 1 - banana
- 1 - handful chocolate chips
- 1 - handful min marshmallows

Instructions:

1. Tear a square bit of foil that is round 12-inch with the aid of 12-inch.
2. Spot stripped banana on foil and reduce it longwise approximately ¾ of the course through. Spread it separated and load up with marshmallows and chocolate chips. Firmly enclose banana by way of foil.
3. At the factor whilst organized to prepare dinner, place wrapped banana on hot Ninja Foodi oven broil or over the hearth for approximately 5min.
4. Take out from the barbecue, open up, and respect!

Nutrition facts:

Calories 228, **fat** 12g, **carbohydrate** 31g, **Protein** 5g.

Ninja Foodi Grilled-Banana Splits

prep times: 5 min **cook times: 4** min **total times: 9** min, **serving: 4**

Ingredients:

- 4 - bananas
- 4 - tbsp. butter
- 1 - pt. vanilla ice cream
- ½ c. chocolate syrup
- 1 - Butterfinger or Heath candy bar
- whipped cream

Instructions:

1. Preheat Ninja Foodi oven broil. Brush cut sides of bananas with liquefied spread, at that point, laid them on hot Ninja Foodi oven broil grind. Cook over medium-high warmth until bananas are brilliant earthy colored and Ninja Foodi oven broil marks appear, about 2min. Turn, skin side down; barbecue until delicate, 2min more.
2. To gather the parfaits, remove the bananas from their skins and mastermind two parts in every one of 4 dishes. Scoop some dessert into each bowl. Shower with chocolate sauce and sprinkle with hacked treats. Enhancement with whipped cream, on the off chance that you wish.

Nutrition facts:

Calories 155, **fat** 3g, **carbohydrate** 34g, **Protein** 2g.

Caramelized Pineapple Sundaes with Coconut

total times: 30 min, **serving: 10**

Ingredients:

- 1 - pineapple
- 2 tsp. vegetable oil
- ½ c. sweetened shredded coconut
- 2½ pt. fat-free vanilla frozen yogurt
- mint sprigs

Instructions:

1. Switch on Ninja Foodi broil. Brush the pineapple jewelry with the vegetable oil. Ninja Foodi oven broil over modestly high warm temperature, turning every so often till the pineapple is daintily roasted and mollified, approximately 8min. Move the jewelry to a work surface and reduce into reduced down portions.
2. In a medium skillet, toast the coconut over slight warmth until awesome, about 2min. Move to a plate to chill.
3. Scoop the yogurt into dessert glasses or bowls. Top with the Ninja Foodi oven-broiled pineapple, sprinkles with the coconut, adorn with the mint twigs, and serve at once.

Nutrition facts:

Calories 214, **fat** 9g, **carbohydrate** 31g, **Protein** 3g.

Grilled Angel Food Cake with Strawberries in Balsamic

prep times: 11 min **cook times: 4** min **total times: 15** min, **serving: 6**

Ingredients:

- 1½ lb. strawberries
- 2 - tbsp. balsamic vinegar
- 1 - tbsp. sugar
- 1 - store-bought angel food cake
- Whipped cream (optional)

Instructions:

1. In a medium bowl, sling strawberries with balsamic vinegar and sugar. Let remain at room temperature until sugar breaks down, at any rate, 30min, mixing at times.
2. In the interim, get ready outside Ninja Foodi oven broil for direct barbecuing on medium. Cut light, fluffy cake into 6 wedges.
3. Spot cake on the hot Ninja Foodi oven broil rack and cook 3 to 4min or until daintily toasted on the two sides, turning over once. Spoon strawberries with their juice onto 6 sweet plates. Spot Ninja Foodi oven-broiled cake on plates with strawberries; present with whipped cream in the event that you like.

Nutrition facts:

Calories 150, **fat** 1g, **carbohydrate** 33g, **Protein** 3g.

CPSIA information can be obtained
at www.ICGtesting.com
Printed in the USA
LVHW101730310820
664660LV00023B/677